Archbishop |

Lenten Lunches

Reflections on the Weekday Readings
for Lent and Easter Week

St. Anthony Messenger Press
Cincinnati, Ohio

Cover and book design by Mary Alfieri
ISBN 0-86716-243-0

Published by St. Anthony Messenger Press
Printed in the U.S.A.

Foreword

These little reflections have their origin in the daily 12:10 p.m. Mass at St. Louis Church in downtown Cincinnati, where I live. Every day a hundred or so people come together there for the Eucharist. Many are office workers on their lunch hour: engineers, attorneys, secretaries, executives. Others are the senior citizens from the nearby apartments— some of which are quite elegant, while others are subsidized housing. We have truck drivers and street people. Occasionally we have some children whose parents school them at home and bring them to Mass during their noon "recess." The 12:10 Mass crowd is a little cross section of the Church.

A few years ago the pastor of St. Louis Church suggested that it might be a good idea to start offering short homilies on the daily Scripture readings, not to exceed three minutes in length. As one who has had the habit of writing everything out beforehand and whose speaking commitments were already considerable, I did not follow the suggestion at first. In addition, my presence at the noon Mass is necessarily irregular due to other commitments around the Archdiocese of Cincinnati. Then I decided to give it a try whenever I was there, and I have found the experience to be profoundly enriching—at least for the preacher! To sit down for a few minutes in the early morning to put together a few thoughts for noon Mass made me more aware of the gift the Church has given us in the weekday lectionary. It has deepened my awareness of the wealth of the Church's liturgical year. It has offered me a chance to be taught in a new way by the Lord and his Holy Spirit.

Now I offer to a wider public some of the fruits of that experience. I hope that what I have been given may be of benefit to others who look for a little added nourishment in their day. These are brief homiletic reflections on the daily readings of Lent and Easter Week (with some slightly extended ones for Ash Wednesday and the Triduum added for the sake of completeness).

These short pieces do not pretend to exhaust the

fullness of God's word in the selections from Scripture or to give a substantial treatment of the implications of the central weeks of the Church's year. They are only a snack for busy people in the midst of busy days.

I offer thanks to my colleagues at St. Louis Church, who have encouraged me in daily preaching and to the members of the congregation who have listened so attentively.

Most Rev. Daniel E. Pilarczyk
Archbishop of Cincinnati

Introduction to the Seasons

Lent

To think of Lent only as a time of penance is to do it an injustice. While the traditional practice of "doing something" for Lent is praiseworthy, there is much more to this wonderful season than just additional practices of piety or acts of penance and mortification. In Lent the Church calls us to *metanoia*.

As a former Greek teacher, I take delight in pointing out that the word *metanoia* connotes a change of mind and heart, altering one's mind-set toward whole new ways of thinking and acting. This involves taking a look at where we are and trying to see where we ought to be. It involves testing our values and discerning how they stack up against the values that Jesus offers his followers.

Fortunately, *metanoia* is not something we have to do all by ourselves. God's word gives us a lot of help in the process, as does the example of our brothers and sisters in the Lord who are engaged, during these weeks, in the same exercise.

Lent is also the season of final preparation for those who will be baptized at the Easter Vigil. The Church invites its members to pray for these catechumens, but also to renew their own commitment to the life that began in them when they were baptized and so became members of God's people.

Finally, Lent prepares us for Holy Week, for those most sacred days in the Church's year when we celebrate the suffering and death of Jesus, the Lord's gift of himself in obedience to the mission he received from his heavenly Father. Of course, the suffering and death of Jesus—and his resurrection—present questions and challenges to each of us in the context of our own mission as followers of Christ and so in our process of *metanoia*.

During the weekdays of Lent, therefore, the Scripture readings for the Eucharist are concerned with three main themes. The selections for the first three weeks have to do almost exclusively with change of heart: what it means and what it involves. They present the classic motifs of Lent: prayer, care for our neighbor, repentance for our sinfulness.

The fourth and fifth weeks offer us a series of selections from the Gospel according to John. These deal at first with the basics of Jesus' mission and thus further outline the change of heart that is required of us while, at the same time, teaching us about what the catechumens--and we—are to seek from him in Baptism. As the season progresses, the readings lead us into the Passion of Jesus, showing us the tensions and controversies that finally led the leaders of his people to do away with him.

Sometimes the Church plays us only one of these themes. Sometimes two or even three of them are presented together in a sort of harmony so that we become aware that a change of heart and beginning a new life and participating in the sufferings of Jesus are all part of what it means to be his disciples.

Easter Time

The weekday readings for the weeks after Easter follow a different pattern than the readings for Lent. In Lent the readings are chosen to complement each other. Both deal with the same basic idea, either by way of contrast or by way of repetition. In Eastertide the Church gives us more or less continuous reading of two books of the New Testament: the Acts of the Apostles and John's Gospel. Each series follows its own path and any correspondence between the two is accidental. In Lent we have duets. In Easter time we have a pair of long solos.

The Acts of the Apostles is the story of the young Church, of what happened after Jesus rose from the dead and sent his Holy Spirit into God's new people. It begins with the preaching of Peter on Pentecost and ends with Paul in Rome, poised to bring the gospel to "the ends of the earth." Like the Gospels, Acts is about Jesus, the risen Lord present in the world through the lives of his followers.

While weekday serial readings from Matthew, Mark and Luke are used in the Ordinary Time of the Church's year, we hear John's Gospel at what we might call extraordinary times, for example, the fourth and fifth weeks of Lent and the whole Easter Season. It's as if the Church wants to give us the more developed reflections on Jesus' life, the teaching of "John the theologian" at times of particular intensity.

Easter week is an exception, however. Acts begins to unfold in the first readings, but the Gospel selections are concerned with the resurrection appearances of Jesus as given by all four evangelists. The Church wants to be sure that we hear all there is to hear in all the Gospels about the risen Christ.

It is these Easter Week Gospel readings that I have chosen to comment on as a kind of dessert course after the six and a half weeks of Lenten lunches. *Buon appetito!*

Ash Wednesday

Joel 2:12-18; 2 Corinthians 5:20—6:2; Matthew 6:1-6, 16-18

Sometimes when the late news begins on TV, a station will run a line of written text across the bottom of the screen: "It's eleven o'clock. Do you know where your children are?" This is a public-spirited effort to remind people that they have responsibilities toward their families.

Today the Church reminds us of our responsibilities: responsibilities toward God, responsibilities toward ourselves, responsibilities toward others. We might imagine a line of text running across the screen of our consciousness today that says, "This is Ash Wednesday. Do you know where *you* are?"

Do you know where you are in relation to the Lord? Do you know where you are in the course of your own life? Do you know in what direction you are headed? Do you know where you want to go? Do you know where you are in relation to other people: coworkers, family, friends? Do you know where you are in relation to the community of believers that is the Church?

We all need to ask ourselves these questions occasionally. When Lent rolls around each year the Church says, "Now is the time to take a look at yourself. Now is the time to see where you are and where you are going." It's good for the Church to emphasize the *now* each year, because otherwise we might be tempted to put off asking ourselves about these things until a more convenient time, and such "convenient" times seem to come rarely, if at all.

In urging us now to ask ourselves where we are, the Church is not just inviting us to engage in self-accusation. The Church is also inviting us to enter a process of repentance, of change of direction.

In Lent the Church does not just say to us, "You know you've done wrong. You haven't been all that you should have been." The Church is also saying to us, "The Lord loves you. The Lord wants you. The Lord offers you forgiveness and mercy to bring you from where you are to where you ought to be." We hear that in the first two readings for today: "Even now, says the LORD,/return to me with all your heart"—to a God gracious and slow to anger, rich in kindness. "Be reconciled to God.... See, now is the acceptable time;

see, now is the day of salvation!"

In the Gospel reading Jesus reminds us that what is asked of us is not a set of external practices but a redoing of our hearts. Almsgiving and fasting and prayer, the classical agenda for Lent, are important, but they are not enough unless there is something going on inside of us as well as on the surface of our lives.

Some practical suggestions: Let your observance of the laws of fasting and abstinence during Lent be a reminder of your own sinfulness and limitations. Pray more. Pray better. You might want to try to get to Mass on all the weekdays of Lent so that you can listen a little more attentively to what the Lord wants you to hear. And you might want to let that question that the Church puts to us today keep running across the bottom of the screen of your consciousness during these next forty days: Do you know where you are?

Thursday After Ash Wednesday

Deuteronomy 30:15-20; Luke 9:22-25

Today we hear for the first time the strains of the passion theme as Jesus tells his disciples what lies in store for him—and therefore for them. But the main melody is about decisionmaking. If we are going to change our hearts, we have to decide what direction we want our lives to take. Otherwise we may just run around in circles.

The Lord seems to know how easy it is for us to do that. That's why Moses, God's spokesman, talks to the people about fundamental options. "You have to decide what you are going to be about. You have to choose whether you are going to go God's way or your way. You must choose either death on your own or life with the Lord."

Then comes Jesus telling us that choosing life means a willingness to give our life away, to be willing to lose it in following him rather than hanging on to it for our own purposes. This saying of Jesus about losing and saving our life occurs some six times in the

Gospels. It must have been a recurrent theme in Jesus' preaching.

A change of heart has to do with choosing. The choices we make determine who and what we are. We can choose comfort or commitment, ambition or generosity, self-serving or self-giving. We make dozens of choices every day, some deliberately and some by habit. But every choice we make has its effect on us. Each one contributes to molding our minds and hearts in a certain direction. And underneath them all is the choice about who will have the central role in our lives: we or the Lord. Today's readings call us one more time to choose God.

Friday After Ash Wednesday

Isaiah 58:1-9; Matthew 9:14-15

In today's Gospel the Pharisees ask Jesus why his disciples don't fast, why they don't reach out for God in the same way that other religious people do. Jesus answers that all his disciples need is right there with them: himself.

Jesus is with us, too, in many ways, but that doesn't mean we don't have to reach for him in fasting and prayer. After all, there are lots of areas in our lives that we don't let Jesus into very often. Sometimes we act as if he were not there at all.

In the first reading Isaiah tells us how we are to reach out to the Lord: not just through certain traditional practices, not just going through a certain set of motions. Seeking the Lord means looking out for our brothers and sisters, the Lord's brothers and sisters. It involves helping those in need. It includes forgiveness and kindness and the pursuit of justice. Then we can look for the Lord and hear him say, "Here I am!"

When you come right down to it, the Lord is never

far away from us. He is in our hearts. He is with us in the Eucharist and in the inspired word of Scripture. He is present in those around us who look for our love and care. In effect, the Lord is all over the place. It is our own inattentiveness that makes him seem distant. It is the walls that we build that make him seem far away.

A change of heart doesn't mean looking into the distance. It means acknowledging what is near.

Saturday After Ash Wednesday

Isaiah 58:9-14; Luke 5:27-32

God can't do much for us unless we realize how much we need God: That's the point Jesus makes in the Gospel today. The "religious" people thought it was terrible that Jesus associated with tax collectors like Levi, whose profession was a kind of legalized extortion. Jesus answers that, if nothing else, the tax collectors were at least willing to find out what he had to offer them. At least they knew that they needed something.

Isaiah continues his discourse on reaching out. We have to look after those in need and put our own personal interests second to our attentiveness to the Lord. It's not just that the needy and the oppressed can't do without our help, still less that God needs our attention. It's rather that those are the ways in which we express our own submissiveness to the Lord. Those are the ways in which we acknowledge that we can't do without God's presence and action in our lives.

We don't like to admit that we need anything. We

prefer to be self-sufficient. Yet that is precisely the mind-set that makes change of heart impossible. Even God cannot change us unless we are willing to accept what God wants us to have, what God alone can give. We may express that acceptance in just wanting to be with the Lord, as Levi and his friends did, or in reaching out to the Lord in the ways that Isaiah mentions.

We won't be healed unless we admit we are sick. We won't be strengthened unless we admit that we are weak.

Monday of the First Week of Lent

Leviticus 19:1-2, 11-18; Matthew 25:31-46

Today's lesson on change of heart is very simple: What we do is important for what we are. Both readings are concerned with our treatment of our neighbor. In the first reading Moses tells the people of Israel how they are to relate to one another. He calls for truthfulness and justice and compassion and love. In the Gospel Jesus tells us that we are responsible for looking out for our brothers and sisters in their needs, whatever the needs may be. None of us is alone. We are all responsible for one another.

But there is a deeper dimension to all this. In the reading from Leviticus there is a kind of refrain that comes at the end of each paragraph: "I am the Lord." "You are to do these things," God says, "not because of what you are but because of what I am. You belong to me. You represent me. I want you to be like me. Be holy because I, the Lord your God, am holy."

In the Gospel Jesus implies that our responsibilities toward our sisters and brothers arise both because *they* are like him and because *we* are like him. Jesus cares for his loved ones through people who are like him looking out for everyone else who is like him. When we care for our neighbor, we act like Christ caring for Christ.

The change of heart that the Church calls us to during Lent is not so much a matter of becoming different than we are as it is a matter of being more effectively what God has already made us to be. Leviticus doesn't tell us to *become* something we are not—holy—but to *be* holy because God is holy.

Tuesday of the First Week of Lent

Isaiah 55:10-11; Matthew 6:7-15

Today the Church gives us a little treatise on prayer, one of the central elements of change of heart. In the Gospel Jesus tells us three important things: The first is that the value of prayer doesn't lie in quantity. The second is that God doesn't need our prayer in order to know our needs. Finally, Jesus tells us what we ought to pray about.

We ought, first of all, to pray about God, about God's holiness, about the kingdom promised to us, about the fulfillment of God's will. When we pray about God we invite the gift of a greater awareness of who God is and what God means—or ought to mean—in our lives and our world. Prayer, then, is not primarily about us. It is about God.

Next we pray about ourselves, about our dependence on God for life, for forgiveness, for perseverance in doing good. Everything that really matters in our lives comes from God.

The reading from Isaiah has a little zinger in it. God

says that no divine word is without its loving effect. Given the juxtaposition with the Gospel reading, God seems to be telling us that, if we pray according to the pattern that Jesus gave us—the prayer pattern from God's own mouth—our prayer will never be without results because in praying that way we are addressing God with God's own words.

Whenever we open ourselves in prayer to a greater presence of the Lord in our lives, whenever we pray about our utter dependence on God, we are sending forth God's words, and God promises that those words cannot be without effect.

Wednesday of the First Week of Lent

Jonah 3:1-10; Luke 11:29-32

When judgment time comes, the people to whom Jonah preached are going to be better off than the people Jesus addressed. At least the Ninevites listened to Jonah, whereas the people Jesus is addressing don't seem to care what he says, even though he is greater than Jonah.

The message that Jonah preached to the Ninevites and that Jesus preached to the crowds is the same message that the Church addresses to us during Lent: "Repent. Change your ways." It's an old message but a message that needs to be repeated in every age because human sinfulness is so persistent. Sin will never be eradicated completely until the time of final fulfillment arrives.

The same sinfulness that was in the Ninevites and in the hearts of Jesus' contemporaries is in us, too. We can never afford to forget that. It's so easy to get comfortable with our sins, so easy to tell ourselves that they don't really matter much. It's so easy to put off dealing with them: "Maybe tomorrow or next week. Maybe next Lent. Not now." Today Jesus tells us, "Now!" The sign of Jonah that Jesus says will be given to the people of his generation is the call to repentance. Jonah's generation responded to it and Jesus' generation did not. Repentance is the test of each generation's faithfulness to God. It is the test of our faithfulness to God also.

Today God lays it on the line with us. "When the day of judgment comes, which generation will you be with?"

Thursday of the First Week of Lent

Esther C:12, 14-16, 23-25; Matthew 7:7-12

On Tuesday God's word told us that we have to pray according to God's pattern for prayer, and that such prayer will never be without its effect. Today God tells us that we have to pray hard.

In the first reading Queen Esther is getting ready to go in to the king to accuse his prime minister of conspiracy. Her life is on the line and she is praying her heart out. She knows how much she needs the Lord's help.

In the Gospel Jesus tells his followers that prayer is something they have to be persistent in. A very literal translation of the Greek text here would be, "Keep asking. Keep seeking. Keep knocking." Prayer isn't something that we do once in a while. It's supposed to be part of the ongoing business of our life.

The reason we have to pray hard, however, is not that God has to be persuaded of our need. God knows what we need and God is so much in love with us that he is anxious to give us what we need. The most loving human parent offers only a pale imitation of God's parental care.

Why, then, do we have to make such a big thing about praying? Why do we have to busy ourselves with prayer so constantly? So that we ourselves never lose sight of how much we depend on God's goodness, of how vulnerable we are without it. We are constantly tempted to self-sufficiency, to thinking that we can get along pretty well on our own. We have to pray hard because, if we don't, we run the risk of forgetting who and what we are.

Friday of the First Week of Lent

Ezekiel 18:21-28; Matthew 5:20-26

The exiles in Babylon liked to think that what they were suffering was the result of their ancestors' sinfulness. Today Ezekiel tells them that's just not so. Each of us is affected by our own virtue or sinfulness. God isn't being unfair if the sinner is punished, because we are all responsible for ourselves.

In the Gospel Jesus also talks about responsibility. We are responsible for what we do. But Jesus goes further than just laying down the minimum: Of course we shouldn't commit murder. But it's also wrong to subject another to anger or abuse. It's wrong to look down on our neighbor. It's wrong to refuse to be reconciled with those who have injured us, real as the injury may be. We have to settle disputes as soon as we can, for fear that they lead us into still deeper waters. We bear some sort of responsibility for every aspect of our relationship with others.

Responsibility is heavy. That's why we have to come to grips with it during a season of change of heart.

It is not that God wants to lay a guilt trip on us today, but rather that God wants us to remember how seriously our Creator takes our freedom and how much God looks for from us. But what God looks for from us can only come as a divine gift.

So we come back still again to our neediness before the Lord, to our dependence on God's goodness to live up to what is demanded of us. A change of heart does not mean that we should begin to scourge ourselves with anxiety and guilt, but rather that we should become ever more aware that we cannot carry our responsibilities alone.

Saturday of the First Week of Lent

Deuteronomy 26:16-19; Matthew 5:43-48

What does God expect of us? If our Lenten change of heart were fully successful, what would we be like?

Today's readings tell us about God's expectations. In the first reading Moses tells the people that they are to carry out all the commands that God has given them with commitment and care so that they can become a people particularly God's own, a people sacred to the Lord.

The Gospel reading is more demanding. Jesus tells us that God expects more of us than just being kind to those who are kind to us. We are supposed to take after our heavenly Father, whose kindness knows no bounds. We are to love as God loves. Nothing else is enough.

That's a pretty high expectation. It's downright frightening if we have to carry it out on our own. But we don't. If God has promised to come to the relief of our neediness in dealing with our personal sinfulness, God is certainly going to provide what we need in order to love as God does. As a matter of fact, we already have that help.

When we were baptized, God gave us the life of Christ to live as our own life. We are no longer limited to our own individual gifts and energies. We have been made over into the image of Christ; we are able to give and to love as Christ did, as Christ does. What the Church's catechumens are looking forward to is already ours.

That doesn't make it all easy, of course, but as persons baptized into Christ we know that we have what we need in order to live up to God's expectations. Change of heart doesn't mean becoming something new, but becoming more effectively what we already are.

Monday of the Second Week of Lent

Daniel 9:4-10; Luke 6:36-38

We continue with our survey course in *metanoia*, a change of heart. For two more weeks the Church will continue to present to us the classic Scripture texts about sin and repentance, about our relationship with God and our neighbor.

Today we hear about retribution. In the first reading we see the prophet Daniel acknowledging that the sufferings of his people are a result of their own inattentiveness to God. In the Gospel Jesus tells us that we cannot expect compassion and forgiveness from God unless we ourselves are compassionate and forgiving. If we are generous in loving, God will be generous with us. If we are not, God will treat us as we have treated others.

It is not that God waits to see how we will behave and then decides whether to be good to us or not, but rather that our own conduct determines our very capacity to receive what God wants to give us. If we are unfamiliar with forgiving others, we won't recognize

God's forgiveness of us. If we are mean-spirited and judgmental toward others, God's generosity toward us won't make any sense. We won't even be aware that it is there. Just as virtue is its own reward, so sin is its own punishment. Retribution is automatic. God simply respects our choices enough to let us take their consequences.

The Lenten change of heart is not an attempt to change God's heart so God will be merciful to us. It is an attempt to change our own hearts so that we are able to receive what God wants us to have.

Tuesday of the Second Week of Lent

Isaiah 1:10, 16-20; Matthew 23:1-12

Today we hear about humility. Isaiah tells us that no matter how bad we have been, how lurid our sinfulness, God will still forgive us if we are willing to admit our wrongdoing and turn back to our Maker. In the Gospel Jesus tells his followers that there is no point in putting on airs. Greatness does not lie in special uniforms or lofty titles; it lies in being willing to serve our brothers and sisters.

Humility does not consist in cringing and wringing our hands and telling everybody that we are no good (hoping, perhaps, in our heart of hearts, that nobody will agree with us). Humility is a matter of being realistic about ourselves. It involves acknowledging that what the world counts as important is not particularly important to God. It calls us to admit that our finest human achievements are shot through with sinfulness and are not all that great anyway. But we are not, for that reason, worthless. We are important to God, not for what we have done or for what we can give, but for what we have received.

And what we have received is the call and the capacity to look out for our brothers and sisters as agents of the loving God. Everything other than that is secondary at best and self-destructive at worst. Greatness lies in service. And humility consists in the willingness to serve. Nothing else matters.

Today God calls us to realism, realism about our limitations and sinfulness, yes, but also realism about the potential for good that is in us through God's gift. God invites us to be exalted— not because we have achieved importance, but because we are willing to serve.

Wednesday of the Second Week of Lent

Jeremiah 18:18-20; Matthew 20:17-28

The passion theme sounds today as we hear the lament of the suffering Jeremiah and find Jesus telling his followers about the cup of sorrow that he is to drink. But these readings are also about us. They remind us that following the Lord involves suffering.

There is the suffering of effort. It's not easy to carry out what God asks of us. It's painful to root out our bad habits and our self-serving attitudes. Sometimes it hurts to give up things to which we have become so deeply attached.

There is the suffering of being different. Committed followers of Christ are increasingly outsiders in this world of ours; it seems that our adversaries are increasing in number and power. If you don't believe that, try analyzing the presumptions that lie behind your favorite TV series and see whether they express the values that we hold.

There is the suffering of being rejected or ignored. Sometimes our best efforts are misunderstood or misinterpreted. Sometimes they are taken for granted. Sometimes they are resented. Sometimes they are not even noticed.

Zebedee's wife and sons thought they knew a good thing when they saw it and they wanted to be sure they got in while the getting was good. It was a good thing that they saw, but it involved something other than they expected. We involve ourselves in a change of heart because we, too, think we see a good thing in our association with Christ. We shouldn't be surprised if the cross is involved.

Thursday of the Second Week of Lent

Jeremiah 17:5-10; Luke 16:19-31

What do we trust in? In what do we find consolation? Jeremiah says that if our trust is in anything other than God we will end up like a barren bush in the desert. Jesus says that if we find our consolation only in what we have here and now we will end up in hell.

It wasn't that the rich man was particularly bad. He was just shortsighted, too shortsighted to see poor Lazarus just outside the gate. The rich man enjoyed all the good things of life and then discovered, when it was too late, that it was he, not Lazarus, who had been in misery.

Lent is a good time for us to look into our hearts and try to see what is important to us. What takes precedence over what? What are we willing to give up for what? When we have choices to make, what criteria do we use to reach a decision? For what are we willing to accept discomfort? For what are we willing to make sacrifices, even little sacrifices?

It's not always pleasant to look into our personal value system. It's not easy, either, because we have such a highly developed talent for self-deception and because we are so easily distracted from the effort. That's why we need to ask the Lord for courage and honesty and perseverance when we come to grips with ourselves. That's why the Church sets aside a whole season each year for us to get to know our hearts so that we can change them.

Maybe, if the rich man of the parable had worked at a change of heart during Lent, he would have ended up differently.

Friday of the Second Week of Lent

Genesis 37:3-4, 12-13, 17-28; Matthew 21:33-43, 45-46

Today's readings are about rejection. We have the story of Joseph, much loved by his father, who had been informed in his dreams that a great calling lay in store for him. So his brothers gang up on him and, in a burst of self-restraint, sell him into slavery instead of killing him as they had planned. In the Gospel parable Jesus describes the treatment that he himself was receiving from those who were in charge of the vineyard of God's people. He knew that, in the end, they would reject him and kill him in order to keep their hold on what they regarded as their own.

These readings are concerned with the passion motif, but they also give us something to think about in the context of change of heart. They deal with those who rejected God's agents, but also with us.

We do not reject Christ knowingly and deliberately. In fact, we rightly count ourselves among those who have accepted him and have given him ourselves in return. Yet our acceptance is often incomplete and limited. Every time we choose ourselves instead of the Lord, even in small things, we give him a little nudge out of the way. When we allow ourselves to become distracted from his service by our daily tasks and the worries that seem so demanding, we are tacitly rejecting him. It's easy to do, given the demands on our attention.

That's why we have to make the effort every year during this season of repentance to see where we stand in relation to the Lord and to realign our priorities. If we don't make that effort, we run the risk of rejecting the Lord—not by decision, but by default.

Saturday of the Second Week of Lent

Micah 7:14-15, 18-20; Luke 15:1-3, 11-32

Today God's word gives us comfort. God is compassionate and forgiving. God removes our guilt, Micah says, and buries it in the depths of the sea. In the Gospel we see just what that means in the parable of the selfish son and the father who loved him so extravagantly.

There is nothing we can do to make our heavenly Father stop loving us. We don't have to deserve God's love by good behavior. As a matter of fact, we can't deserve God's love. It is simply there for us from the beginning and remains there no matter how far afield we may wander. However unfaithful we children may be, God remains our loving Father.

But we do have to accept our Father's love, not because God needs credit for being a loving Father, but because we need to realize how precious we are to God. If the selfish son had stayed on the pig farm, the father would have loved him still, but the son would have remained alienated and in misery. He had to come home to experience how much he meant to his father.

Lent is a season of homecoming. The Church calls us to recognize that we have all drifted away, maybe to a far country, maybe just around the corner. None of us is everything we should be. We all need some degree of reconciliation with our Father.

Lent is the ideal time for a really good confession— not so that God will find out what we have done, but so we will realize how selfish we have been and so that we can hear, personally and individually, that God loves us anyway and that we are still welcome in God's household.

Monday of the Third Week of Lent

2 Kings 5:1-15; Luke 4:24-30

When Jesus returned to Nazareth after the beginning of his public ministry, the people of the town looked for big things from him. They had heard about his miracles and expected that he would certainly want to show the folks at home what he could do. Jesus is not a magician, however, but a prophet with his own agenda, and that agenda doesn't necessarily include preferential treatment for friends and relatives. As was the case with Elijah and Elisha, the prophet's horizons may be wider than local people expect.

The first reading relates the Naaman incident that Jesus alludes to and shows us, in passing, that even those who are the objects of the prophets' kind attentions sometimes want to tell them how they ought to go about their mission.

These readings allude to the passion theme and remind us that Jesus met hostility from the very beginning of his career. But they also teach us that God's mercy is unconditional and universal. God doesn't just look out for those who think they have some claim on divine mercy because of past faithfulness. You don't have to "belong" in order to qualify. God cares even for "outsiders."

The point for us is that God's forgiveness and mercy are offered to us not because we deserve special treatment but because God is God. None of us has a claim on God's attentions. To the extent that we are sinners and members of a sinful people we are all outsiders. Yet God cares for us anyhow. In our process of change of heart it's important for us to remember precisely why God pays attention to us.

Tuesday of the Third Week of Lent

Daniel 3:25, 34-43; Matthew 18:21-35

Today we hear some more about forgiveness. The first reading shows us Azariah in the fiery furnace in Babylon. He acknowledges that he and his people have been brought low by their own sinfulness and prays that a change of heart will evoke God's mercy. In the Gospel parable Jesus teaches us that God's mercy is indeed available, but only to those who are themselves merciful and forgiving.

Forgiveness is hard because it involves loving other people in spite of the evil that they have done to us. When we forgive, we don't deny the hurt that we have received. We don't deny that it was wrong. We don't pretend that nothing happened. But we acknowledge that there is more to the offender than the offense. It's that *more* that we acknowledge when we forgive; it's that *more* that we love in spite of the offense.

We need to forgive those who have harmed us for two reasons. The first is that God has forgiven us so much and so often for our offenses that the refusal to do likewise to those who have offended us is nothing short of pettiness. The second is that God has made us over into the image of Christ in Baptism and so expects us to love—and to forgive—even as Christ loved and forgave. Forgiveness is not just one more item on God's agenda for us, but rather a consequence of what God has made us to be. We are called to love as generously and as universally as God loves, in spite of how people may have treated us, just because we are what we are.

Whom are you called to forgive?

Wednesday of the Third Week of Lent

Deuteronomy 4:1, 5-9; Matthew 5:17-19

Today's lesson is simple: Obey the Commandments. We hear Moses telling the people that their observance of the Commandments they have received from God will be evidence of their wisdom and intelligence. Then Jesus tells the crowds that they should not look on him as someone come to offer a new system of commandments, but rather as one come to raise the old ones to a new level of fulfillment.

There are two important issues here: The first is that the Commandments are gift, not burden. They are not a series of tasks, like the labors of Hercules, with which God tests us to see whether we are faithful or not. They are, rather, the directions God gives us so that we can live and function most productively in accord with what we were created to be. Those who follow these directions show themselves to be wise and intelligent.

The second issue is that Jesus' teaching puts the Commandments into a whole new dimension. They don't just guide us to live *our* lives most successfully.

They also guide us to live *God's* life that is in us. Those who live in Christ are called to function as an extension of him and so to live a life of total reverence for God and of total love and service to their brothers and sisters in the Lord. In many ways, the external behavior of Jesus' followers may be the same as that of others who are trying to do the right thing. But the source and meaning and goal of that behavior will be different.

Today's readings raise two questions for those engaged in a change of heart: How well do I observe the Commandments? Why do I observe them at all?

Thursday of the Third Week of Lent

Jeremiah 7:23-28; Luke 11:14-23

The Italians have a proverb: No one is more deaf than the person who chooses not to listen. Today Jeremiah rebukes the people because they didn't want to listen to the voice of God, to the prophets. Jesus says the same thing to those who were deliberately misinterpreting his miracles. "The only reasonable explanation of what I do," he says, "is that I am more powerful than the forces of evil. But you insist that I do what I do because I am in league with the devil. You refuse to understand my works because you have chosen not to understand me."

Most of us do not deliberately reject what God wants us to hear. As believers, we strive to understand and respond to what the Lord tells us in his word and in his Church. But our level of attentiveness often leaves something to be desired.

We have lots of things to distract us: our families, our jobs, our worries—not to mention the constant background noise that our culture provides for us. In addition, there is the nagging suspicion that, if we are too attentive to the Lord, we may hear the Lord saying things to us that we might not want to hear: an invitation to be less dependent on the crutches of comfort, a call to come to grips with our failings, a reminder that we have some forgiving to do.

This is where prayer comes in. More than saying words, prayer is quiet attentiveness to the Lord, clearing away some of the clutter in our lives so that God can get through to us. Renewed attention to prayer is one of the central agenda items of Lent. During these weeks, God says to us, "Turn up your hearing for a while and listen to me."

Friday of the Third Week of Lent

Hosea 14:2-10; Mark 12:28-34

Today's readings are both dialogues. Hosea tells the people that if they will just express their willingness to turn to God, the Lord will respond with healing and love and abundance. "Tell me you love me so I can show how much I love you," God says in effect. The Gospel is a discussion of the basic commandments between the scribe and Jesus. They agree that loving God and loving neighbor are the foundation of our relationship with God. We can almost hear their enthusiasm as they share their convictions about the most basic matter of all.

Being loved by God and loving in return: That's the central axis on which everything else rotates, the central necessity to which everything else must refer. Our relationship with God is not an affair of keeping hundreds of little regulations, but of coming to know how much God loves us and of responding in kind both to God and to those whom God loves. Living out the relationship may often seem complicated and demanding. We sometimes find it hard to see how love is to be expressed in our concrete circumstances. Sometimes carrying out the requirements of loving seems to demand more than we can readily give. But the center of it all is quite simple: to accept the love God offers us and to give it back every way we can.

One of the great saints has said that at nightfall, when our life is coming to a close, we will be examined in love. Each year at Lent the Church reminds us that we have to be serious about preparing for that final exam.

Saturday of the Third Week of Lent

Hosea 6:1-6; Luke 18:9-14

Today we have two eloquent speeches. Hosea shows us the people in prayer, exhorting one another in moving words to rely on God's care for them. In the Gospel we have the Pharisee grandly reminding God what a great saint he is and how much he does for the Lord. Neither speech is very effective. In the first reading God rejects the prayer of the people because their faithfulness is as insubstantial as morning fog. Jesus says that the tax-collecting racketeer is closer to God than the pseudo-saint because at least he knows how much he needs God's mercy.

One of the greatest temptations of all is to think that God will pay attention to us if we just say the right words and that we can earn God's kindness to us if we just do enough good deeds. The malice of that kind of attitude lies in the presumption that it is we who are in charge and God who reacts to us. If we think that we have the wherewithal to make God love us, we are living not in a dream world but in a nightmare world in which everything is turned upside down and inside out.

Holiness does not consist in how much we do for God or in how eloquently we speak to God. Holiness consists in what God does for us and in how open we are to accepting God's gifts. That's the lesson that God offers us today as we come to the end of the third full week of Lent.

Metanoia, a change of mind and heart, involves getting things in right order. What we need to get right is who is in charge and who is in need of whom.

Monday of the Fourth Week of Lent

Isaiah 65:17-21; John 4:43-54

Today we begin the second half of Lent. The general survey course on change of heart with which the season began now gives way to a series of readings from the Gospel of John, with Old Testament selections chosen to correspond with them.

These Gospel readings are concerned, in part, with the theme of Baptism. They talk about what those who will be baptized at Easter can expect from Baptism. At the same time, they remind us who are already members of the Church of what we have received from the Lord. They also gradually lead us into Holy Week and the Passion of the Lord.

Today's readings are about life. Isaiah speaks about the abundance of life that will come when God's will has reached fulfillment. Jesus saves the life of a royal official's son, a boy who is at death's door.

The underlying point is that God has made us not to die but to live. Isaiah uses extravagant language to express this point when he says that, in the day of the

Lord, anybody who doesn't reach one hundred will be thought to die young. Just as the royal official didn't want to lose his son, so God doesn't want to lose us. God loves us so much that he wants to have us around forever, fulfilled and energetic, enjoying all the capabilities he has so generously given us.

That's why our heavenly Father gives us the life of Christ in Baptism. As long as we maintain that life, we will live as Christ lives, glorified and complete. Death is not a conclusion but a point of passage into something far better that will never end. It's good to be alive when the life you live is the life of Christ.

Tuesday of the Fourth Week of Lent

Ezekiel 47:1-9, 12; John 5:1-3, 5-16

Today God talks to us about healing and abundance.
The vision of Ezekiel is about abundance. God's
gifts are not given with an eyedropper but in rivers, like
a flow of clean water abundant enough to make
seawater fresh. And one of those gifts is healing of both
body and soul, as Jesus healed the paralytic by the pool.

Of course the reference to water in both readings
encourages us to think about Baptism. Jesus has healed
us in Baptism, healed us of the spiritual disabilities that
come from our inherited sinfulness. Once we are
baptized, we are no longer disabled people, crippled
with sin. We are made over, new and energetic in the
life of Christ.

Sometimes we don't feel very new and energetic.
Sometimes it seems that we are still spiritually
handicapped as we strive to walk the path of our life.
The deficiency, however, is not in the gift of new life
that God gives us but in ourselves. Often we inflict new
weaknesses on ourselves by our personal sins. Often we

suffer from the results of past sinfulness, our own sinfulness or that of others.

Most of the time, though, our apparent disabilities come from our unwillingness to accept the abundance God has given us. We are afraid to walk in the Lord. We think that if we take seriously the Lord's command to get up and walk, we will fall on our faces. We are more convinced of our own limitations than we are of the Lord's generosity. Wouldn't it have been sad if the paralytic had said to Jesus, "Thanks, but I'll just stay where I am"?

Wednesday of the Fourth Week of Lent

Isaiah 49:8-15; John 5:17-30

Liberation means freedom from limitation, from
constraints that keep us from what we might
otherwise do and be. Today God's word promises us
liberation. In the words of Isaiah God promises, in a
time of favor, to free us from imprisonment, from
hunger and thirst, from the obstacles that keep us from
traveling onward. In the Gospel Jesus offers to free us
even from death if we believe in him.

The point is not that people of faith don't have any
problems and will never have to experience death.
Rather, the point is that, if we live in the Lord, the things
that seemed to be burdens will prove to be blessings,
and death will prove to be a passage to a new kind of
life.

Death comes to believers and unbelievers alike.
Even Jesus had to die. The difference is that those who
have accepted the life of Christ are ready at death to
enjoy the kind of life that Jesus entered at his
Resurrection. The others are not. They are stuck with

the lesser things that they put their faith in, all of which are meaningless in the realm of the Lord. They are unable to experience liberation because the only thing they were ever interested in was their chains.

God liberates us at Baptism. When we are baptized we begin to live the life of the Lord, a life that cannot be limited by any earthly constraint. Our lives as believers consist in the continual response to that liberation, in making it ever more our own. Because we live in Christ we are free. Just how free we will be when our physical death comes depends on how serious we are about our freedom now.

Thursday of the Fourth Week of Lent

Exodus 32:7-14; John 5:31-47

The readings today and for the rest of this week begin to lead us more directly into our commemoration of the passion and death of Jesus. They deal with the reasons why the leaders of Jesus' time wanted to put him to death.

Today John tells us that Jesus was rejected because people refused to recognize him for who and what he was. We see Jesus presenting his credentials. He reminds his hearers that he is teaching the same things that were taught by John the Baptist, who was recognized as a man of God. Then there are Jesus' miracles, which indicate that even God is giving testimony to the validity of Jesus' mission. In Jewish law, two witnesses were enough to establish truth.

But there was more. Moses had said that God would send another prophet like him (see Deuteronomy 18:15), and Jesus' people were looking for such a prophet. Jesus now says that he is the one they are looking for; he is the successor to Moses. Those who knew Jesus knew that he was a leader, that he wanted to bring people into touch with God, as Moses did. After his death on the cross, it became clear that Jesus was also an intercessor for the people as Moses was on the mountaintop. (The first reading recalls this incident.)

But those who should have known better refused to accept Jesus' credentials. They chose to believe that he was an impostor and eventually drove him to death.

Jesus' credentials are the same today as they were then. Today Jesus asks us whether *we* accept those credentials or not.

Friday of the Fourth Week of Lent

Wisdom 2:1, 12-22; John 7:1-2, 10, 25-30

Why did the contemporaries of Jesus want to put him to death? Because he wasn't just like everybody else. In today's Gospel we hear Jesus telling his critics that they don't know as much about him as they think they do, that he has a relationship with God that they neither understand nor share.

The reading from Wisdom tells us what happens to people who make such claims. They constitute a threat and an accusation to those around them. The goodness of the just one highlights the wickedness of the others, who react by trying to get rid of the just. It's dangerous to claim to be close to God.

As baptized persons we share the life of Christ, so we shouldn't be surprised that we sometimes encounter rejection and hostility. There's no need to be paranoid and imagine that the whole world is out to get us, but the fact remains that we have different values, different goals, different ways of acting than many people in the world around us. And people don't like to be told, even implicitly, that they are wrong. Sometimes their reaction to us is expressed in a sharp comment or a sneer, sometimes by a joke, sometimes by downright meanness. It doesn't happen often. Maybe it even happens too seldom.

We have been refurbishing the image of Christ in us during Lent. Here's a question we might want to ask ourselves in view of today's readings: If it were a statutory crime to be a follower of Christ, would there be enough evidence to convict us?

Saturday of the Fourth Week of Lent

Jeremiah 11:18-20; John 7:40-53

One reason the leaders wanted to put Jesus to death was the following he was beginning to attract. While some continued to wonder about him, others were convinced that he was the prophet like Moses who had been promised or even the Messiah. The police who had been sent out to arrest him came back empty-handed because they, too, were impressed by Jesus. Finally, when Nicodemus—one of their very own number—comes to Jesus' defense, the conclusion seems clear. Something has to be done about Jesus.

In the first reading we hear Jeremiah reflecting on his own situation. These words could almost be the reflections of Jesus as he saw the net closing about him. "Father, be with me. It's not just my cause that is at issue here, but yours, too."

The readings of these days teach us that the execution of Jesus was not something that the leaders of the people decided on in an instant of misguided panic. They had heard him and seen him over a long period of time. It became ever clearer that this man was dangerous. On a number of occasions throughout the ministry of Jesus they had decided to get rid of him. But they had to wait for the right opportunity.

When the time came, Jesus was not taken by surprise. He knew what they had been thinking and planning, and he probably could have gotten away from them had he wanted. But he stayed on his mission, faithful to his calling to the last, even when it was clear that it would cost him everything.

That's the kind of faithfulness God expects from us, too.

Monday of the Fifth Week of Lent

Daniel 13:41-62; John 8:1-11

Today's readings are filled with contrasts. There is the obvious contrast between the innocent Susanna and the guilty adulteress. There is contrast between the dirty old men in the first reading and the righteous religious leaders in the second (who, nonetheless, seem to be lusting to punish the adulteress and entrap Jesus). There is contrast between Daniel's demand that the legal requirements of evidence be observed more exactly and Jesus' strategy to demonstrate that the requirements of the law call for more than mere literal execution.

But there is a common element in the readings, too, and that common element is mercy. Mercy means kindheartedness, care and compassion for those who are in trouble. By sending Daniel in response to Susanna's prayer, God showed concern for her seemingly impossible situation. By making the accusers of the adulteress realize that they, too, were sinners, Jesus brings them to see that even those who have done wrong still deserve compassion.

Mercy is important for all of us because we all need mercy from God. As we pray during these weeks for those who will be baptized, we recall that none of us deserves salvation. None of us can earn it. It comes to us as a free gift from a merciful God. As we continue our process of change of heart, we remember that even after our Baptism we have sinned; God has every reason to write us off and forget about us. But instead of that, God offers us mercy. A change of heart involves gratitude. Today we thank God for the divine mercy.

Tuesday of the Fifth Week of Lent

Numbers 21:4-9; John 8:21-30

Today, tomorrow and Thursday the Gospel readings are from the eighth chapter of John's Gospel. They are part of a long discourse in which Jesus tells the people who and what he is. The people get increasingly frustrated with him and, at the end, they are ready to stone him. These readings speak to the baptismal theme of Lent because they deal with Christ, in whose image the baptized will be recreated, and they speak to us who are in the process of renewing our relationship with him.

Today Jesus says that he really belongs to another world. He calls himself by God's name, I AM, and then compares himself to the bronze snake that Moses lifted up to cure the people of their wounds. He will be the source of salvation because he comes from the Father.

We haven't been bitten by serpents in the desert, but we are all wounded nonetheless. We are wounded by the sinfulness that we have inherited. We are wounded by the hurts that our own sinfulness has inflicted on us.

The only one that can cure us is Christ, who forgives and heals with the power of God. Today the Church invites us to look up to Christ, lifted on the cross, to acknowledge our sinfulness and to renew our trust and hope in him.

Lent is coming to a close. Next week we will live again the suffering and death of Jesus. We continue our work on *metanoia*, changing our hearts. It's appropriate to ask ourselves how far we have come and what agenda items still lie before us if our heart is to be changed. Have you made a good confession yet this Lent?

Wednesday of the Fifth Week of Lent

Daniel 3:14-20, 91-92, 95; John 8:31-42

In the first reading we hear how God liberated the three men from the fiery furnace. There was no power that could have saved them except God, who sent an angel to rescue them from the most powerful king on earth.

Today Jesus calls himself the great liberator. His hearers reply that they don't need any liberation because they are descendants of Abraham. Therefore they enjoy all the blessings that God promised to Abraham—blessings that no sort of political oppression could take away from them. Jesus replies that, if they are in sin, it doesn't matter who their father is. They are still slaves to sin. The people then reply that their real father is God, and Jesus answers that God can't possibly be their Father if they don't accept the one God has sent to free them.

Jesus liberates us, too, from whatever forces hold us in slavery. It's not just that Jesus forgives our sins through the sacraments of Baptism and Reconciliation, although he does that. Even more, Jesus offers us new values, new goals, new purpose, new energy in our life. We are no longer subject to earthly powers, whether those powers be self-seeking or comfort or distraction or dependency. He frees us from every kind of fiery furnace because, after Baptism, we don't live just our own life anymore, but his life, which will never lessen and never end.

That doesn't make everything easy. We still have to struggle with our chains. But our struggle is not to achieve liberation, only to accept it. If the Father of Jesus is our Father, nothing can enslave us.

Thursday of the Fifth Week of Lent

Genesis 17:3-9; John 8:51-59

For the Jews, there was nobody quite like Abraham. He was the father of the people, the man who was in touch with God, the one to whom God promised everything: land, prosperity, a special relationship with God for himself and his descendants. Today's first reading shows us God in contact with Abraham, a contact that was repeated and renewed throughout his life. Abraham was God's man *par excellence*.

Now comes Jesus, claiming that he can offer more than was given to Abraham and that somehow Abraham looked up to him. Again he identifies himself by calling himself by God's own name: I AM. Either Jesus was himself God or was an outright blasphemer. Those who heard him there in the temple thought he was a blasphemer and got ready to execute him by stoning, as the law prescribed. It was not the last time they would try to put him to death. Eventually they would succeed.

We, on the other hand, believe that Jesus was God.

We take him at his word. He is the fulfillment of the promises made to Abraham, the founder of God's final people, the one who will free his people even from death, God in person reaching out to us with God's own life.

These readings help us understand why Jesus ended up on the cross. They remind us of the life that comes to us through Baptism. And they call us to renew our hearts and minds at the deepest level of our relationship with God: the level of faith. Everything that we are and do is determined by how we stand with Christ, by whether we accept him or reject him. These last days of Lent are a good time for us to renew our determination to be true to him, to be true to his word.

Friday of the Fifth Week of Lent

Jeremiah 20:10-13; John 10:31-42

More threats today. The people want to stone Jesus because it is becoming ever clearer that he is claiming to be God. Jesus answers that Psalm 82 calls the leaders and judges of the people "gods" because of the authority they exercise. If they are gods, why can't Jesus be God? It's almost as if he is trying to argue himself out of a tough spot. But then he goes on to argue himself right back into it by saying that his sonship is quite different from theirs, and so they come after him again.

The faith of Jeremiah echoes the consciousness of Jesus: "My enemies are all around me but I know that you, O God, will save me because I am yours."

We live the life of Christ through Baptism. We, too, are sons and daughters of God—not because of any role or responsibility we have been given, like the Old Testament leaders called "gods" by the psalm, but because we have the same relationship to the Father that Jesus had. We are God's children not because of what we do but because of what God has made us to be.

Everything else is secondary to that. Human suffering, human success and failure, wealth and poverty, popularity and rejection: All are trifles compared to the basic relationship that makes God our very own Father. And only we can undermine that relationship through our inattentiveness, through our pursuit of other values, through our sins.

As we approach Holy Week and the celebration of the passion and death of Jesus, God's word makes clear who he is. God's word also invites us to remember who we are.

Saturday of the Fifth Week of Lent

Ezekiel 37:21-28; John 11:45-57

In the final analysis, Jesus died for the good of God's people. The cynical Caiaphas says in today's Gospel that that's how it has to be, but, as the evangelist points out, he is saying more than he realizes. Jesus dies not just to maintain public order, but to bring the people into a whole new level of relationship with God.

This is what Ezekiel describes: one people, gathered in from everywhere, cleansed from their sins, obedient, living with God forever in God's own land under the leadership of the son of David.

The death of Jesus marks the culmination of his life of faithfulness and dedication to the will of his heavenly Father. In Jesus a human being had finally lived the kind of life that God had intended us all to live. A human being had been all that God intended us all to be. His faithfulness costs Jesus his life, but then comes a new kind of life, a glorious and fulfilled risen life that will never end.

That's the life that we share through Baptism.

Because we are in Christ, all of us together form a new people, gathered in from everywhere: a people faithful like Christ, obedient like Christ, citizens of a new promised land. For us Christ carried his mission to its conclusion, even to death on a cross. Christ died for his people so that his people can live in him.

In the Opening Prayer for today's Mass the Church prays that God will protect all those who are about to become God's children and will continue to bless those who are already baptized. It's good for us to enter Holy Week mindful of who we are and how we became what we are.

Monday of Holy Week

Isaiah 42:1-7; John 12:1-11

In these first three days of Holy Week the Gospel readings are about the last days of Jesus' life. They tell us that he knew that the end was near, that Judas would betray him, that the other apostles would run away from him.

The first readings are the first three Suffering Servant Songs from Isaiah. (We will hear the fourth on Good Friday.) The Servant Songs are a series of poems written during the Jews' exile in Babylon. Like all great poetry, they have various levels of meaning. Sometimes they seem to be about the prophet himself, sometimes about the people as a whole, sometimes about the ideal Israelite who sums up the past yet leads the people to a new future. From the earliest New Testament times, believers have seen Jesus as the embodiment of Isaiah's Servant of God. During these last days of Jesus' life, the Church offers us the Servant Songs as a kind of poetic meditation on the person and mission of Jesus.

In today's Song we hear that the Servant is endowed with the power of God. He will not be a revolutionary political leader, but will work quietly, with compassion for the weak, the sightless, the oppressed. His mission is to bring the justice of God to every part of God's creation.

That's how Christ has dealt with us. He has been patient with our weakness. He has given us a new kind of vision. He has freed us from the oppression of our sins. He has brought us into a new Kingdom that stretches to all the earth and extends even into heaven.

Today we thank our heavenly Father for his Servant. Today we thank Jesus for his self-sacrificing faithfulness to his mission.

Tuesday of Holy Week

Isaiah 49:1-6; John 13:21-33, 36-38

Today we hear about the calling of the Servant. God
had plans for him before he was born. God prepares
him as a warrior prepares his sword and his arrows.
Even though it seems at times that his work is useless,
God is with him, helping him bring the people
together—not just the people of old but a new people
who will extend God's salvation to the ends of the
earth.

The life and mission of Jesus were not some last-
minute idea on God's part. Right from the beginning,
after the sin of Adam and Eve, God had promised to
overcome the forces of the devil. Then God called
Abraham to father a people who would be ready to
accept the divine gift of salvation. God freed them from
their exile in Egypt and sent them prophets to keep them
aware of the divine plans for them. Everything that
happened to them was somehow connected with the
ultimate Servant, the one who was to come, the prophet
like Moses. Even their rejection of the Servant when he

came couldn't frustrate God's plans. Out of the Servant's suffering and death God brought about salvation for the whole world.

Our life is not some sort of chance happening either. God has had plans for each of us from long before we were born, and those plans have their meaning in our association with the Servant of the Songs. They may include suffering and uncertainty, but they are still God's plans. Like Jesus, each of us has a cross to carry, but each of us is called to ultimate success. The Servant of the Songs is Jesus but, because we are in Jesus, the Songs are also about us.

Wednesday of Holy Week

Isaiah 50:4-9; Matthew 26:14-25

The Servant of the Songs is familiar with suffering. He accepts it without resistance, without counterattack. He has listened to God, morning after morning, and he knows that his enemies are not going to have the last word because God is with him.

We see this same attitude in Jesus in today's Gospel. He calmly makes arrangements for the Passover supper, knowing all the while that his time of suffering is drawing near and that he will be handed over to his enemies by one of his own. There is no attempt to escape, no provision for resistance. He is ready to suffer what he needs to suffer in order to bring his mission to its completion.

We have suffering in our lives, too. Sometimes it is physical. Sometimes it is mental. Sometimes we inflict it on ourselves. Sometimes it comes to us through betrayal by those we have loved or trusted. But it is there. We do what we can to deal with it because we know that God wants us to exercise care for ourselves, but there is always something left over that we are unable to eradicate, always some hurt that will not go away. We don't understand why this needs to be so, but we know that another Servant has suffered before us. And we know that God is powerful enough to bring blessings out of our suffering even as God brought salvation out of the sufferings of Jesus.

We are coming to the end of the Church's annual call to increased self-awareness and repentance. One of the things we learn again in these last days is that we are never without the Lord, and that, even when we have a cross to carry, we carry it with Christ.

Holy Thursday

Exodus 12:1-8, 11-14; 1 Corinthians 11:23-26; John 13:1-15

The most basic lesson of Jesus' life in general and of his passion and death in particular is that the value of a human life depends on giving it away, in spending it on something other than ourselves.

Throughout the years of his public life Jesus spent his time teaching and healing, walking the roads of Judea and Galilee, offering his word and his power and his presence to all comers, friends and enemies alike. It wasn't a comfortable life or an easy life. Yet he kept at it because he wanted to make clear through his life that our worth is not in what we get but in what we give. That's how the Father wanted human beings to live from the beginning. That's the lesson that human beings needed to relearn after generations of sinfulness and selfishness. That's what the life of God's incarnate Son was meant to demonstrate.

On the occasion of the last meal with his followers, Jesus taught his lesson still again. When he washed the feet of his apostles, it was to get them to realize one more time that the important thing is to care for others rather than to be cared for by them. "I have set you an example, that you also should do as I have done to you." And then he taught the lesson of giving in still another way. He gave them himself under the appearance of bread and wine. He gave them himself to be their energy, their motivating force, their life. Jesus' whole human existence was a process of giving himself away and he summed it all up at the end when he washed his followers' feet and gave them the Eucharist before he went out to make the final gift of his life on the cross.

Jesus' lessons are for us, too. We are naturally inclined to look after ourselves first, to seek happiness and fulfillment according to our wishes, in accord with our wants. But Jesus teaches us, as he taught the people of his own time, that happiness and fulfillment must not, cannot be pursued directly and for themselves. They are by-products that come as a result of forgetting about happiness and self-fulfillment, of forgetting about ourselves. Jesus teaches us that we are most ourselves when we look out for ourselves the least, that we get the most out of our life when we give away the most.

The lesson of Jesus' life is offered to us every day in

the Eucharist. Jesus gives us himself—not in some "merely symbolic" way but in his total reality: body and blood, soul and divinity. He gives us himself not just so that we can have a little visit together each day but so that we can gradually grow more and more into him and more and more like him.

Jesus gives us himself so that we will become ever more capable of giving ourselves—of giving ourselves in patience to those who annoy us or even injure us; of giving ourselves in service to those in need, whatever the need may be; of giving ourselves in comfort to suffering people around us; of giving ourselves in obedience and submission to the will of our heavenly Father. We speak of receiving Christ in the Eucharist and that's correct. We do receive him really and truly. But we receive him in order to become him and we seek to become him in order to spend ourselves as he did. Nothing else is important.

Good Friday

Isaiah 52:13—53:12; Hebrews 4:14-16; 5:7-9; John 18:1—19:42

As we reflect on the events that are recorded in John's passion narrative, it is only natural to ask ourselves what Jesus' death is all about. What does it mean?

From one point of view, it's quite simple. Those who oppose Jesus gather a crowd together and scare the Roman governor into letting Jesus be executed. Jesus is an innocent man, done to death by his more powerful enemies. But there's more to it than that.

For one thing, Jesus is done to death because of his message—a message of God's love offered to all human beings. This message simply seemed too good to be true. It seemed dangerous to the power brokers. Jesus could have backed off. He could have toned down his message. He could have gotten out of the country or simply kept quiet. But he didn't, and the reason he didn't was because the message was too important.

The Good News of God's love was—and is—a message that everybody needs to hear. It's a message that gives ultimate meaning and purpose to the life of every human being. If Jesus had backed off, he might have saved his life, but the message would have been lost. Jesus remained faithful to his message even when he began to see that it would cost him his life. He died so that the truth he preached would be available to the people of his time, so that it would be available to us. Jesus died for his message, the message that is our salvation. Jesus died for us.

But there is still another dimension to Jesus' death. He was sent from his Father with a mission, and that mission was not just to teach, important as that was and is, but also to demonstrate what human life is all about. Jesus came into a world like ours, a sinful world, a selfish world, a shortsighted world. Through the whole course of his life Jesus showed that the real value of human life lies in relationship to his heavenly Father. Everything Jesus did was directed to the love of God and to the love of those who are loved by God. His mission was to live human existence as God had intended it to be lived from the beginning. He remained obedient to that mission even when it cost him his life.

From then on human life has been different in God's sight. Sin and selfishness and shortsightedness remain, but God now offers a whole new relationship to those who are willing to continue the life of Jesus, to those who are willing to live with the values and goals and relationships that were his. Our life is different because we share the life of Jesus. Our life has a new depth because Jesus was faithful to his heavenly Father even when that faithfulness brought about his death. Jesus died for us.

These are deep and complex matters. Isaiah looked forward to them in the fourth Servant Song. The Letter to the Hebrews reflects on them in terms of Jesus' reverence and obedience. Yet like all the greatest truths, this one can also be expressed very simply: Jesus died for us. That is what we celebrate today.

Easter Vigil

The Easter Vigil is the richest and most complex liturgy of the Church's year. Light and darkness and water and music all have their part to play. We hear a long series of readings from Holy Scripture. Next come Baptism and Confirmation and the Eucharist. On this night we are celebrating not only Jesus' resurrection from the dead but also the liberation of the children of Israel from Egypt. It almost seems that there is too much going on. We are inclined to feel input overload.

Yet there is a common theme to it all that ties it together into one understandable whole: God's purpose. That's what the readings are about. God created the earth, called light out of darkness and created humankind in the divine image for a purpose. God called Abraham to the mountaintop for a purpose. God freed the Israelites from Egypt for a purpose. God takes extravagant care of God's people, as we hear in the readings from Isaiah, and it is for a purpose. God raised Jesus from the dead for a purpose. Nothing that happens in the Creator's relationship with human creatures takes place by chance. There is a purpose, a reason for everything.

And the purpose, the reason for it all, is so that God can love us. God made a world so there could be human creatures to love. He called Abraham and tested him so that Abraham could experience God's special love for him. God freed a people because of love, so that they could experience that love in a land of their own where God could take special care of them. God sent us Jesus and ultimately raised him from the dead so that there would be a whole new level of life for us to enjoy: Christ's life, the life of the one human being who lived in full accord with God's purpose, a life that will never decline and never end.

In Baptism and Confirmation God increases the membership of the people he loves so specially. In the Eucharist God strengthens the life of Christ given to us so that we can love God more deeply and so that there will be more in us for God to see and love. And in all this God prepares us to take the divine love beyond our Christian community into the world that God wants to make ever more perfect and ever more receptive to love. It's all connected with a purpose, the fundamental purpose of everything: God's purpose of loving the strange and wonderful creatures we are made to be.

Lots of people spend their lives without much sense of purpose, just getting through one day at a time, never asking or knowing why. Others set up purposes and goals of their own, and when they reach them, they find that they aren't much wiser or much better off than before—and then they start all over again. But those who have come to know and respond to God find that there is purpose in every aspect of their lives, that there is nothing without meaning, and that the horizons of that purpose and meaning stretch far beyond the hassles of today into the realm of the risen Christ.

It all fits together: God's interventions in human history; the life and death and resurrection of Jesus; our life—past, present, future, individually and as Church. It all fits together under the overarching, comprehensive, determined purpose of God to love us.

Believers know that there is always a *because* and that the ultimate *because* is "because God has chosen to love us." And that is what we celebrate at Easter.

Monday of Easter Week

Acts 2:14, 22-32; Matthew 28:8-15

The Gospel readings this week are from all four evangelists, two each from John and Luke, one each from Matthew and Mark. They all have to do with the appearances of Jesus after the Resurrection.

It's hard to fit all these accounts into one coherent narrative or to understand exactly what happened on each occasion. The reason is that they are not intended to be an hour by hour, day by day history. Rather they are the memories of people who were involved in something so wonderful they couldn't quite grasp it at first—memories collected and written down thirty or forty years after it all happened.

But there are several elements that are either explicit or presupposed in each of the accounts. First, there is no body in the tomb. In spite of the attempt on the part of the authorities to explain away that absence, as we hear in today's Gospel, it becomes clear that the reason why there is no body was that Jesus isn't dead anymore. He has risen. Second, Jesus appears to his followers. The order and the circumstances of the appearances are not all spelled out, but everybody who talks about the Resurrection in the New Testament says that people who had known Jesus when he was alive saw him after he had risen. Finally, it is the same Jesus, body and all, yet somehow gloriously transformed—so different that sometimes people don't recognize him at first.

The risen Christ is still with us today, not in a visible form, but no less real. And he stays with us for the same reason he came to his disciples then: Jesus loves his followers so much that even death can't keep him away from them. That's pretty good news for a Monday.

Tuesday of Easter Week

Acts 2:36-41; John 20:11-18

Today we have a spectacular case of mistaken identity. Mary Magdalene is at the tomb trying to figure out what has happened. She is convinced that someone has stolen the dead body of Jesus and she intends to find it. So she goes after the gardener. Then he speaks her name, and it all becomes clear in an instant. The gardener isn't the gardener. That body hasn't been stolen. The body isn't dead. The body is alive and it's Jesus. She embraces him, but he asks her not to hang on to him because there is still more to come. He sends her back to the others to give them the news about what has *really* happened.

Two points for us here. First of all, if we want to encounter Jesus we have to be looking for him. He's present to us in lots of ways: in the Church, in the sacraments, in Scripture, in our sisters and brothers, in our times of companionship with them in prayer, in the quiet life he lives in our hearts. But we have to be attuned to his presence and his voice. If we're not looking and listening, all we will find is tombs and gardeners.

Second, our encounters with Jesus are not just personal matters between us and him. Just as Jesus didn't settle down for a nice long chat with Mary Magdalene but sent her to bring the news to the others, so we, too, are sent to spread the news of the living Christ. By the way we live and work and relate to other people, by the values we profess and the goals we pursue, we are called to testify that we, too, have seen the Lord.

What passed between Mary Magdalene and Jesus on that first Easter is something that still happens all the time.

Wednesday of Easter Week

Acts 3:1-10; Luke 24:13-35

Today's Gospel presents a question: Why didn't the two disciples recognize Jesus? After all, they had known him before his death and now they were in his company, not for an instant but for several hours. But still they didn't know who he was till the end. Perhaps it was because Jesus didn't want them to recognize him by the ordinary means that we use to recognize people: physical appearance, tone of voice and the like. He wanted them to learn to recognize him in a new way, by different means.

So he presents himself to them as a fellow traveler, open to being part of their company. He brings them to see that they could find him in Sacred Scripture if they only knew how to read it properly. Finally, he breaks bread with them, and the truth dawns at last. Then he disappears, as if to say that he didn't need to stay around in his old, humanly recognizable form, now that they knew where else to look for him.

This little story is not just about those two disciples

on the first Easter. It is about us. The risen Christ offers us his company in our brothers and sisters as we walk our journey. He speaks to us in the inspired word of Scripture. Best of all, he offers us himself, really and truly present and active in our midst, whenever those who believe in him break the eucharistic bread in his memory. The point of the story is that the risen Christ is no longer limited to the dimensions of his earthly life. He maintains contact with his followers in wonderful new ways. He is with us here. He is with us now.

Thursday of Easter Week

Acts 3:11-26; Luke 24:35-48

It was hard for Jesus to get his followers to understand what was going on. Here are the two disciples explaining what had happened on the road to Emmaus, but the others don't believe them. And when Jesus appears in their midst, they think they are seeing a ghost.

Patient teacher that he is, Jesus goes to great pains to demonstrate that he is not a ghost, but someone real and alive—real enough to bear the wounds of his suffering, alive enough to eat a Sunday evening snack.

Then he goes on to teach them some more. He helps them to understand that what had happened to him was not the result of human scheming, but was part of God's plan from the very beginning. It was meant to be that way, and what God meant to accomplish isn't over yet. The salvation Jesus came to bring is for the whole world. These disciples are to be the agents for getting the word out. They are to be witnesses of the truth of Christ.

The plan that God brought to partial fulfillment in Jesus isn't over now, either. It's still unfolding, thanks to the continued presence of the risen Christ in the world, thanks to the testimony of those who believe in him. We are part of that plan, just as the first disciples were.

It's important for us to remember that Jesus is alive and real. It's important for us to remember that the rest of the world is not going to know what that means unless we keep finding ways to tell them.

Friday of Easter Week

Acts 4:1-12; John 21:1-14

Today we see the risen Jesus helping the apostles at their work. He indicates where the fish are to be found and they recognize him when they see the abundance of their catch. They haul in 153 big ones— just about every kind there is—yet the nets hold up under the weight.

The point of this story is that the task to which Jesus called his first followers, to be fishers of souls, continues even after his Resurrection. They are still to work as they did before, only now the risen Christ will be helping them and the results will exceed the capabilities of the means they use. Just as no net can ordinarily include every kind of fish without breaking, so the apostles themselves will not be able to carry out their mission to the whole world without the assistance of the risen Christ.

Jesus did not rise from the dead just to offer personal reassurance to the small number of his followers who actually saw him. He rose from the dead to complete and continue the mission he had begun in his public life. He was to draw everybody to himself, to bring the whole world into contact with his love. And the community of the believers were to be his agents.

Today's Gospel is about the Church, which continues the harvest of souls that Jesus began. In many ways, it's an impossible task, given the fragile human means at its disposal. Yet the risen Christ is involved in it, too. "It is the Lord" who guides the Church and guarantees its productiveness. He is with us still.

Saturday of Easter Week

Acts 4:13-21; Mark 16:9-15

We come to the end of Easter Week with a reading from the Gospel of Mark. This reading is a kind of summary of the appearances of the risen Christ in the other Gospels: to Mary Magdalene, to the two disciples on the road, to the other followers. And the message that Jesus offers is the basic message of the Resurrection: Believe and proclaim.

Believing and proclaiming has been going on in our selections from Acts all week. It will continue throughout the Easter season as the Church reads on through this account of what the apostles believed and proclaimed.

The whole history of Christ's people is the history of belief and proclamation. Throughout its entire life the Church has been striving to be faithful to the command of the risen Lord: Believe and proclaim. That's what the Church is still engaged in today.

In Lent we came to grips with changing our hearts to be more faithful to the Lord. We walked with those who were to be received into God's community and with Jesus as he moved toward his suffering and death. At Easter we were with the disciples as they came to understand that Jesus was with them still in his new and glorified life. And now we move forward to carry out in our world and in our time the command that the risen Christ gave to his first followers: Believe and proclaim.

Jesus has been with us during these weeks, and he will be with us always. It is he in whom we believe. It is he whom we proclaim.